CW00369860

INTRODUCTION

Parrots of the world have always fascinated humans because of their often flamboyant plumage, famed longevity, and renowned intelligence. This interest dates back as far as the times when we first started to form social groups and live in organized settlements or encampments.

As a group, the parrots display a greater range in size than any other group of popular avians. They are also among the select few birds that are able to mimic sounds, including that of the human voice. They are mainly indigenous to the warmer areas of the world, where they are found in a range of habitats from arid desert terrain to lush tropical forests.

Many parrots, including this Salmon-crested Cockatoo, are now close to becoming endangered or are already so. It is very important that anyone who owns one of these beautiful creatures do everything in his power to propagate the species before they are lost forever.

SCIENTIFIC STATUS

Parrots are housed in the zoological order of birds called Psittaciformes. In species number, they represent only about 3.5 percent of avians (there being some 9,000 bird species, but only 330 parrots). Because of the accumulative effect of habitat destruction for roads, mining, human settlements, and mass capture for the pet trade, as well as destruction because of their crop feeding habits, many members of the order are tottering on the brink of extinction.

The order of parrots is divided into three broad subdivisions known as families. There is Loriidae, housing the 55 lory species, Cacatuidae, the cockatoos with just 18 species, and Psittacidae, the true parrots with 257 species.

Parrots are readily distinguished from all other birds by the shape of their beak, their colors, and the way they perch. They are often known as hookbills, because their larger upper mandible, beak, or bill curves downwards in the manner of the birds of prey. They perch with two toes facing forwards and two backwards, this known as being zygodactyl; birds of prey have three toes facing forwards and one backwards. Unlike the raptors, the diet of parrots is almost totally of plant matter in its various forms.

DOMESTIC HISTORY

It is almost certain that the Egyptians kept parrots, but little has been recorded about their involvement with them; the same being true of the early Asian and Chinese cultures. What we do know is that Alexander the Great, on his eastern conquests, took parrots back to his Macedonian (Greek) homeland. This introduced the people of Europe to these birds. Thereafter, they became firm favorites in the homes of the Greek, Roman and all other Empires. The Spanish conquistadors introduced the many gorgeous parrots of South America to Europe, while the British colonization of Australia brought the magnificent parrots of that land mass to the attention of parrot enthusiasts the world over. The first people to introduce non-indigenous parrot species to the USA were the South American Potcheca traders. These ardent natives regularly trudged north as far as Arizona and New Mexico—even to Kansas and present day San Francisco, and possibly further north. They took with them many macaws and other South American species to trade as pets, and for their brilliantly colored feathers which were used by the Indians in headdresses. Mass remains have been unearthed in settlements dating back to 900 A.D.—500 years before the arrival of the Spanish to that continent.

Although parrots have been kept as pets for many centuries, ownership tended to be very much within the more wealthy homes. This changed dramatically following an event in March of 1861. Two ships, the Orient and the Golden Star out of Adelaide, had docked in London carrying a total of three thousand pairs of budgerigars. Britain's most famous animal dealer of the time, Charles Jamrach, purchased all.

By the 1920s this tiny little grass parakeet had won the hearts of many thousands of devoted owners, and opened the door for the many other parrot species to follow in its wake. In respect of numbers, these would be the cockatiel and the numerous species of lovebirds. Following the end of World War II, the larger parrots

Parrots were captured and taken to other countries to become pets as more lands were explored and conquered. Today, many countries do not allow the export of their native birds. This is a Yellow-tailed Cockatoo in its wild habitat of Australia.

started to gain in popularity, especially those which were either very colorful and good aviary breeding birds, or those which had talking potential.

THE CHANGING TIMES

In looking back in time to the mid 1900s, there have been many changes within the parrot hobby. At that time most species, other than the three already mentioned, were captured from the wild and sold at what were relatively low prices. It was as though there was a never ending supply. But in 1959 the Australian government placed a ban on the export of all of its native flora and fauna. Its effect was dramatic. The price of Australian parrots rapidly increased while much greater efforts were placed on establishing breeding pairs and colonies of those in captivity. It also increased the popularity of African, Asian, and South American parrots, which could still be obtained from the wild at low prices. However, Australia's ban proved that supplies could be suddenly cut off.

The Western World was becoming increasingly aware of the need to conserve its wildlife, and the underdeveloped countries were also becoming aware that they should not allow the continued rape of their natural resources. More countries started to ban the export of their precious avian jewels. The beautiful Plum-headed parakeet of Asia, once one of the least costly of parrots, started to become less seen and more costly. Cuban parrots become all but impossible to obtain, and many of the Latin American parrots also started to climb in cost as restrictions were placed on their export. The wise parrot enthusiasts concentrated on breeding and hand rearing youngsters. This has greatly advanced the hobby because today there is no need to risk purchasing what might be an old, wild parrot of very questionable character. The domestic bred parrot, from every possible viewpoint, is superior to its wild counterpart as a potential pet or aviary breeding bird.

As a first time owner of one of these enthralling birds you are therefore very fortunate when compared to parrot owners of yesteryear. You have more healthy birds from which to choose, more commercial foods available, considerably more appliances and cages from which to choose, and an extensive range of magazines, books, and specialty clubs to help you establish yourself within the hobby.

In this work the thrust of the text is directed towards advising you on the most crucial subjects—selection, feeding, housing, training and care. In the final chapter a number of the more popular species are described, and you are advised to select your first pet, aviary display, or breeding birds from that selection.

A breeding pair of Cuban Amazons in their wild habitat.

THE RIGHT PARROT FOR YOU

Possibly the most common error that many pet owners make is selecting a pet that proves to be totally unsuited to their needs and expectations. In such instances, it has to be said that such owners really have only themselves to blame. Clearly, they made few, if any, inquiries about the species they purchased. They listened only to the good news related to that pet while burying in their minds the potential drawbacks.

Let us carefully look at every aspect of parrots so that your chances of selecting the right one for your needs are greatly increased. Indeed, you should first consider whether a parrot is in fact suited to you. If it is, you need to ponder and discuss with other family members living in your home what sort of parrot you would all like. This decision made, you then need to know what age to purchase at, where to buy from, how to assess good health, and what sort of price range you will be looking at relative to other parrots.

Be sure you have considered all aspects of owning a parrot *before* you purchase one. Things such as the bird's life span, amount of attention time, and how loud a certain species can be, must all be taken into consideration.

You know this is the sensible way to go about things. Do not be unduly influenced by what sort of parrot your friends may have, or how a salesperson may try to persuade you to purchase what they have, rather than what you want. At the end of the day you are not your friend; your situation may be totally different to his. Likewise, you are the one who must live with your choice—the salesperson doesn't!

IS A PARROT THE RIGHT PET FOR YOU?

Before all else, your first thoughts should be focused on whether you are suited to a parrot or not. All psittacines are intelligent and very social birds. All are very inquisitive and acrobatic. These facts mean they are only suited to people who can devote quite a bit of time to them. They thrive on attention; if this is missing, they become very sad pets. In such instances they will need the company of their own kind, which in turn means much larger accommodations, and a reduced one on one relationship with their owner.

Parrots should be allowed out of their cage on a regular basis. This means there is the distinct

Do not choose a species of parrot solely on its looks. There is a large variety of very attractive birds available that can offer you a lot of affection and friendship. This is a Sun Conure that enjoys having his head scratched.

possibility they can get into mischief. They may nibble on woodwork, knock the occasional ornament over, or chew on anything they think looks interesting and potentially edible. They will of course void some fecal matter, although a specific area designated for this activity may be offered. The extent of their activities will of course reflect their size, which should always be a major consideration.

It has to be said that the older owner should also give some thought to the fact that many parrots are quite long lived. A cockatiel, for example, may exceed 20 years. This is by no means long by parrot standards, many attaining two or three times this age. What will happen to the pet if it outlives you? Give this considerable thought prior to purchasing one of these long lived species.

CHOOSING THE RIGHT SPECIES

Although many parrots will not be available to you, either because they are not seen in captivity, or because they are so rare as to be prohibitively expensive, this still leaves a very large number to choose from. Many owners make bad decisions due to misconceptions, or lack of forethought, which they quickly come to regret. For example, you should not assume that all parrots have the ability to mimic the human voice well. Never purchase one of these birds primarily for this reason. It suggests that the owner is more concerned in having a pet purely to use as something to impress friends with than for the companionship these avians can provide. Few parrots have sweet melodious call songs. Most emit a rather raucous sort of sound, this being especially so of the larger the species under consideration. The moderately sized Amazon can offend a neighbor some houses away while a macaw can be heard for a considerable distance when it decides to announce its presence!

In choosing a suitable species you must take into account its voice and where you live, otherwise you could become very unpopular with neighbors. It is within their rights to complain to local authorities about the noise level.

Another aspect that needs careful thought in relation to the size of the parrot is the power of its beak. One of the smallest members of the order—the lovebirds—can inflict a painful nip, so you can imagine what the larger species can do if they are frightened or badly handled. If very small children are in your home, the medium to larger species would not be advisable. You can work on the assumption that the larger the species, the more costly, noisy, potentially destructive, and less suitable it will be in the average home—and most certainly to the first time

Yellow-headed Amazons have a reputation of being excellent talkers. Some have even learned to sing opera! If you have very close neighbors, the amount of noise a parrot like this can make may not be appreciated.

A parrot's bite can be quite destructive. Their hook-type beak can cause a lot of damage. Be very careful when young children are handling such birds. Adults should always be close to supervise.

parrot owner. Do not think, as many beginners do, that the smaller the parrot the less "parrot" it is. All of these birds exhibit all of the features associated with their group, it being the case that some just happen to be smaller than others.

Certain parrot groups are better suited to aviaries than as home pets. Many of the Australian parakeets are examples of this, and are also among the most beautifully colored, so are seen at their best in aviaries. The terms parrot and parakeet are appended to many species, but these have no scientific meaning. In common usage, the term parrot is usually applied to species with short tails. Parakeets have long tails, but are still parrots, and the large macaws have long tails, but you would not call these parakeets!

Another misconception that could result in obtaining an unsuitable parrot is related to their feeding habits. Many first time owners are under the mistaken belief that parrots subsist on a diet essentially made up of various seeds. This is quite incorrect. The lories, lorikeets, and a few other species must have nectar as well as seeds: this makes their fecal matter very liquid. Their cage is often quite messy if it is not cleaned on a very regular basis. The tropical parrots need a goodly selection of fruits in addition to seeds to maintain prime condition. Only certain of the Australian parakeets can survive quite well on mainly a seed diet, but even these should have fruit and other plant matter included. You should therefore check the nutritional needs of the species you are interested in prior to making a purchase.

Taking all of these factors into consideration, the best choice for the first time owner is definitely within the medium to smaller species. Those that go out and purchase large macaws or cockatoos invariably have good reason to endorse the adage of "buy in haste, repent at leisure!"

AGE TO PURCHASE

With but a few exceptions, if you are purchasing a parrot as a pet it is always best to purchase a young bird. This brings with it numerous advantages. Such a bird will become hand tame far quicker (if it is not already so), will make a more endearing pet, will be easier to train, will be healthier, will be less likely to bite, will be quieter, and of course, will live for a longer time with you than an older bird.

The problem with any mature parrot is you cannot be sure of its age unless it carries a year-dated, closed leg band. These are normally seen only on the smaller species. Some breeders do not use bands because they fear the chicks may get the bands caught and injure themselves; others fear the hen may attempt to remove the band, hurting the chick, or even throw it out of the nest. Without a year-dated band, you must trust the word of the seller. With an older parrot, you cannot know for sure why it is being sold, and so must assess the seller more carefully. Maybe it is very destructive to furniture, or it screeches for no apparent reason. It may be a biter, or one that is extremely nervous. Of course, you can get some idea of its nature by how it reacts to your approach, and if it can be handled, but not to the other possible negatives. Of course, the young bird will be more costly, but this cost really is worth every cent for the more superior pet you will obtain.

Macaws are known to have a life span in excess of 50 years. It is not uncommon to find older birds offered for sale due to an owner's death or some other misfortune. Such birds can be very loving and adaptive to a new home, however, they can also be very loud and destructive. Investigate thoroughly before you bring one home.

Captive-bred, hand-raised baby parrots are very common. These birds make excellent pets because they know nothing except being handled and cuddled by humans from practically right out of the egg.

A straight from the nest baby is the best choice with the smaller species, or a hand-reared bird of the medium to larger parrots. The earliest selling age of the youngster will depend on the species.

Sometimes a parrot (usually the medium to larger ones) is sold because the owner can no longer keep it for any of many reasons. The bird may be a very genuine and super pet, but you will not know this until after you have bought it, so there is an obvious element of risk involved. This type of mature bird is best purchased from a specialist bird or pet shop, where you can normally obtain a "return if not satisfied" warranty with it.

If you are looking for display birds for an aviary, or for breeding purposes, the age is not quite so important. Indeed, young or even mature adults may often be more desirable for other reasons such as breeding.

WHERE TO PURCHASE FROM

The best place to obtain your parrot will be influenced by the species you want, and the reason you want it. Your choice is between bird or pet shops and breeders.

Pet shops

Some stores specialize in birds exclusively, so these will normally have the largest selection and the most appliances. The average pet shop will tend to stock the smaller species, and maybe just one or two larger parrots. This outlet is mainly geared to providing pets rather than breeding birds, and is the most convenient outlet for the average pet owner. If you are looking for a particular species they will often be able to locate it for you from one of their suppliers. Prices will be variable, but competitive. You should shop around.

Breeders

If you need quality breeding or show stock you will need to locate an aviarist who specializes in the species you want. Such an aviary may not be local to you, so you may have to purchase via mail order, or undertake a lengthy trip.

Bird specialists advertise in all of the avicultural magazines. You should also visit foreign bird shows that have parrot classes, or an all-parrot show. Pet shops and commercial aviaries may have stock for sale at the larger shows, apart from which you can see more species at this location than at any other single source. It is obviously the best place to contact breeders.

ASSESSING AGE AND HEALTH

In order to have a better chance of telling whether a given parrot is very young, or not, you must read as much as you can about the species you are interested in. Some parrots are in mature plumage before they are one year old, others can be two or more before this is the case. Once adult, it is all but impossible to determine age, so you are left with the honesty of the seller. In general, if you see enough examples of your favored species, you will be able to tell which are obvious youngsters. Some pointers are as follows:

Cockatoos will often fluff up their feathers to appear larger than they really are. They will do this in play or when they feel threatened. A bird can tell you a lot about its personality through its body language.

1. The eye of a youngster will tend to look larger in comparison to its head size than will that of an adult. Its eye color will not be as obvious as that stated for the adult.
2. The beak or bill will be much smoother on a baby than on an adult, the color often not being quite as defined as the adult.
3. A baby's leg scales will be very smooth and may not be as large as on the adult.
4. A young bird's plumage will not be as vivid. Certain wing, tail, or head markings may not be evident until it has passed

through its first full molt.

5. Generally, a baby bird will have the look of a youngster about it, but this you may not be able to appreciate until you have seen many examples. You are reminded that in some species the juvenile male resembles the adult female.

In assessing health, you should first take note of the conditions the birds are living under. Cages should be spacious and not overcrowded with stock. Food and water containers should be very clean, not such that it is obvious they were not washed for days. The cage floor should be quite clean. Perches should not be badly worn and caked with hard fecal matter.

The cage bars should be clean, as should the surrounding area in which the birds are kept.

If a bird is sitting with good, tight feathers, has no discharge from either the eyes or beak, and is active, it is in good health.

Sometimes parrots of different species are housed together for company. Generally, it is best that species not be mixed, especially if they are young birds, and most certainly not if they are of considerable difference in size.

Satisfied as to general cleanliness, you can now focus on the birds. If it is wanted as a pet you really should insist on a hand tame youngster. If the seller is loathe to handle it, this is not a good start, regardless of the excuse given! Normally if the bird is young it will be tame—very much so if it is hand reared.

The eyes should be round and clear with no signs of weeping. The nostrils should look normal, and not in any way swollen or clogged with mucus. The upper mandible will fit neatly over that of the lower jaw with no suggestion of being maligned. The latter is more likely to be seen in the very commonly bred species such as budgerigars, cockatiels and lovebirds, than in the larger parrots. It is undesirable in any member of this order.

The anal region should be clean and not stained or clogged with fecal matter. The toes should all be present on a potential show specimen, but in a pet a missing toe is not a major problem. These sometimes get bitten off during inter aviary squabbles. Though not desirable, a missing toe will not impede a pet.

Some parrots, for example budgerigars, can suffer from a condition known as "going light." This displays itself by the bird having little muscle on either side of its sternal keel—the breast bone. It is thought to have a nutritional base. Such birds should be avoided because it is not easily overcome.

The plumage should lay flat to the bird and display obvious good condition. An occasional missing or bent feather is not a problem, it will be replaced at the next molt. Birds with feathers

The plumage of a bird should display obvious good condition. Open each wing and examine under it for good feather and no skeletal impediment.

looking very bedraggled, however, should be passed over. A healthy parrot will have no areas with missing feathers. Some head plumes may be missing in young birds because their parents may have plucked these. If body feathers are missing, this is a different matter. The cause may be parasitic or fungal and such birds should be overlooked.

Missing feathers can also indicate a condition known as feather plucking, in which the bird denudes itself. In a young parrot the cause is likely to be a nutritional deficiency, but in an older parrot it may be the result of boredom. It can be difficult to cure this habit, so these birds should be left where they are.

If a bird is seen to display signs of parasites, mites and their like, there is a better than 50/50 chance others in that establishment may also have them. This suggests another supplier should be sought. Any form of lump or swelling is clearly indicative of a problem, especially on a young bird. Open each wing to check that these are in good feather, and that the wing itself is quite normal and showing no signs of malformation or other skeletal impediment.

Only if you are totally satisfied as to the health and nature of a parrot should you consider its purchase. There are so many nice parrots to be had that there really is no need to buy one that is either untamed, or in any way less than what you are looking for. Such birds are usually purchased by those unwilling to pay the higher price of a quality pet, or who just lack the patience to look elsewhere. Be prepared to wait for just the right bird.

THE MATTER OF PRICE

The cost of a parrot can range from a modest few dollars to thousands. In general, the larger the species the more costly it will be. However, even within the same species, prices can range considerably. You should be aware of the factors that will influence prices. When comparing one bird with another you must be sure you are comparing like with like, not one person's price against another.

Baby birds do not have very good balance. This takes time and practice. When removed from their nest or brooder, a low perch should be placed in their accommodation to help them become coordinated.

1. A young hand reared bird will be more costly than a straight from the nest youngster, which in turn will be more expensive than an older juvenile.
2. A domestic-bred bird will be more costly (and desirable) than an older, wild-caught imported specimen.
3. The more unusual color mutational forms will be more costly than normal, wild type colors. In some species, such as Asian parakeets, this will be especially so.
4. Exhibition quality birds will be expensive compared to their pet equivalent.
5. Rare parrot species will obviously be expensive. They are best used for breeding purposes rather than as pets (the latter really being a needless waste of such birds).
6. Regional price variations can be expected in all countries.

From the discussions in this chapter, you can appreciate that there is much to ponder before you go out and buy your first parrot. Do not forget that in your financial planning you should allow for a cage of good quality, and of a size appropriate to the species kept. This can be quite an item in itself if you opt for the larger species, another good reason for starting with the very popular and smaller parrots with which you can gain experience.

HOUSING YOUR PARROT

Given the vast difference in the size of parrot species, it is clear that the type of housing must reflect this size in its space, materials used in its construction, and in its fitments. The range of parrot cages, in both style and cost, from which you can choose these days is quite bewildering. In this chapter, we can look at the features you should be looking for in any cage, regardless of the species it will house. Likewise, the main considerations of a good aviary will be reviewed.

When deciding which parrot species is best suited to your needs, you should also ponder your cage needs for some time before you actually purchase one. Certainly, you are advised to obtain the cage *before* you purchase the bird, assuming you have fixed on the upper limit size of the parrot you want. This will give you the time to shop around and compare styles and prices, as well as the fitments that

The type of housing you purchase for your new parrot should be large enough to allow it plenty of exercise room. Elaborate designs are not necessary.

you may wish to include in the cage. You can reflect on the best site for the cage in your home, as this may influence the ultimate choice and size of the cage.

You may find the cage you prefer is rather more costly than you had planned, so you have the option to delay purchasing the bird while you save the extra cash needed. Once the cage is on hand, you can take your time in seeking just the right bird.

CAGE SIZE AND STYLE

All too often you will see parrots housed in cages that are far too small for them. Do not make this fundamental error. Your choice of cage should follow a minimum guideline. Its height must be such that when the adult bird is on the highest perch there is still at least 5cm (2in) of space above its head, and when on the lowest perch there should be at least the same amount below its tail feathers.

Do not clutter your bird's cage with a lot of toys. More room will be more appreciated by your parrot than a lot of toys that always get in its way.

There must be enough space that when the bird is perched centrally and fully extends its wings, neither wing will touch the cage bars in any direction. Anything less than this is too small. A cage can never be too large, so the more space you can provide the better. Remember also that length is more important than height, especially for the smaller parrots. With regard to style, the shape should be a rectangle, thus providing length. The old bell style parrot cages are the least desirable and should be avoided, as should any that are tall and round. These are ornamental and serve no practical needs whatsoever for any bird. All cage bars should be parallel—avoid those where the bars converge at a given point. Your pet might get its beak, or even its leg, stuck between the bars where they converge. Also, check that there are no sharp metal ends protruding into the cage on which your pet might injure

The cage you purchase should allow you to be able to reach inside of it without any struggling or other movements that might upset your parrot.

itself. Look at the quality of all welded joints. Joints that are not smooth can be a source of harboring parasitic eggs. The bars themselves should be of a thickness appropriate to the species, and ample cross members will allow the parrot to climb up and down with ease. The better quality cages will have a generous chromium plating that will stand up to the attention of your pet's beak. Low cost units will have a much shorter lifespan: they will soon begin to rust. Some cages have a colored epoxy resin on them which enables you to select a color that coordinates with your room.

Never get carried away with design features that are more ornamental than practical. The cage door should be large enough to permit easy access for you and the bird. It should have a fastener that cannot be opened by these intelligent avians. In some models, the entire side can be dropped to form a large platform, in others the door may serve the same purpose. Yet others have a top that opens to create this facility. Some cages are built so the base can easily be detached, and this makes for easy cleaning—the easier cleaning is, the less likely it will be ignored, or postponed for days at a time.

A well designed cage will have food and water pots that can easily be replenished from the outside. There should be a sliding base tray so the cage is readily cleaned with minimal inconvenience. The better quality cage will have an external

Round cages do not accommodate birds very well. They do much better in square or rectangular shaped cages. If you do purchase a round cage be sure it is large enough that the bird does not hit the sides of it while exercising its wings.

Table-top play areas or perches are available from your local pet shop. They come in a variety of sizes and styles to accommodate the species you keep.

sloping apron for seed husks, bits of fruit, and feathers to be channeled back into the cage, rather than fall onto the surrounding floor.

Very large cages should be on small wheels so they can be moved around. Smaller units are best placed on a very solid surface if they do not come complete with secure legs. A minimum of two perches should be featured in any worthwhile parrot cage. These should be sited at slightly different heights, and with a suitable distance between them so the bird can exercise its wings as it moves from one to the other. Never clutter a cage with toys and other things that might impede exercise space.

The best perches to obtain are those which have a variable diameter along their length. These

When housing several birds together at one time, ample room must be allowed within the cage so that the birds do not fall over each other.

metal rings for the birds to clamber up, others with ladders, and a matrix of perches. You can purchase ropes and rings from your pet shop and thread these through pieces of hardwood to make an enjoyable toy that the bird will clamber up to nibble on the wood. Avoid using chains because birds can get their toes caught in these with injurious results.

Give your pet pieces of fruit branches to play with. It will strip and eat some of the bark (which is good for it) and the branches are easily replaced at little or no cost. Spent wooden cotton bobbins are another item that will amuse your parrot, as will any of the commercial seed blocks and tonics produced these days. The more of

provide much better exercise for the pet's feet than straight perches. If your pet can close its foot entirely around the perch it is too small and its claws will soon become overgrown.

PARROT PLAYTHINGS

Pet shops today sell an extensive range of toys and other parrot playthings, but a word of caution is appropriate. Be sure that the toy is suited to your species. Fragile plastic budgerigar toys will soon be demolished by lovebirds and conures. If bits are swallowed (unlikely but possible) they could prove dangerous, even lethal.

The best plaything for a parrot is a climbing frame fitted with a food station. There are many models to select from, some with ropes and

No cage can ever be too big for the species you keep. If your parrot will only be away from its cage for short periods of the day, it is important that his cage be extra spacious.

its own toys it has, the less likely it will seek things to nibble on elsewhere in the room.

INDOOR FLIGHT CAGES

The indoor flight cage has become much more popular in recent years, a result of which a number are now made commercially. Some models are no more expensive than the higher priced parrot cages, so they represent excellent value if you have the space for them. They provide much more scope for you to furnish them with natural branches, climbing frames, and so on. Be sure the one you select has wheels so it can be readily moved and is, like the cage, constructed of materials that will

There are many play things available for your pet parrot. Most are made of chewable materials that allow your bird to destroy them over time. Be sure that the type of toy you purchase is safe for the type of parrot you keep.

Cockatoos are very destructive birds and only the hardest of play toys should be provided within this type of parrot's cage.

stand up to the rigors of your pet's beak.

SITING THE CAGE

Give careful thought to where your cage will be sited. It must not be facing a door through which cold drafts could chill the bird. Nor should it be placed next to, or above, heating or cooling units that could create either excess heat, cold, or rapid fluctuations in temperature as the unit goes on and off.

Parrots enjoy basking in sunshine, but they must always be able to retreat from this at their choice. Place the cage such that this is facilitated—a cover over one part may be the answer. It is better that the cage benefits from the early morning sunshine than that at midday, when the temperature is at its highest.

Your pet will enjoy being placed outdoors in its cage on warm days, and will revel in light showers. But never leave it in direct sunshine for other than short periods, nor in downpours. Of course, if the cage does get wet it must be carefully cleaned afterwards so rusting does not occur.

AVIARIES

If you are thinking of building one or more aviaries for parrots, you are advised to seek out larger works that discuss these in greater detail. Any for other than the smallest species will be very costly to construct. They must be extremely robust to withstand the power of a medium to large parrot's beak. You must also take into account the potential noise that aviary parrots can make. Local planning permission may be needed, and any services provided, such as water or electric, must meet federal and local standards of safety.

It is crucial that aviaries are planned very carefully so they are sited in the best position to take advantage of early morning sunshine, yet be protected from cold winter winds and driving rain. Avoid placing aviaries under trees as these carry many more negatives than benefits. Be sure the aviary is not sited over sewage, water, or electric cabling that you may need access to in the future.

The length of the actual flight should be as long as possible, and especially so for the Australian and Asian parakeets, which are strong flyers. Part of the flight, that nearest the birdroom or indoor shelter, should be covered so the birds can remain in the flight, but have some protection from both sunshine and rain. The pop hole that connects the flight to the shelter should have a door that can be closed without your having to enter the flight.

Never leave any exposed wood, even for budgerigars, otherwise the aviary frames will soon be whittled away. The flight panels are best made in sections so they can be conveniently replaced or repaired. The hole size and weldwire gauge will need to be chosen with care so they are appropriate to the species. Where aviary flights have a common weldwire face, it is prudent to double wire it so birds in adjoining flights cannot bite the legs of those in the next flight. Many injuries, even deaths, are caused by this every year.

If the aviary flight has an external door this should be protected by a safety porch—which is also suggested for the door to the birdroom. Fit strong padlocks to these, and the birdroom door because unfortunately, parrot thefts have become a sad reflection of the society we live in. A night light is another useful security device that is simple and low cost, yet quite effective.

The floor of the flight should be such that it can be hosed clean. This means it cannot be of bare earth. Concrete, slabs, or a

Outdoor aviaries can be very attractive and enhance one's garden's area. An aviary for a parrot must be constructed of the hardest materials because most of these birds prove very destructive over time.

generous layer of gravel chippings are your best options. There should be a slight slope away from the shelter so rain will quickly disperse.

From an esthetic viewpoint, it is best that the flight height be in excess of 6.5 ft. It should be painted in black bitumen which will help mask and preserve the weldwire. Do not clutter the center of the flight with branches and perches. Place these at either end so your birds have maximum uninterrupted flight space.

The birdroom should be well insulated, while the provision of electric, water, and sewage will be worth every cent in enabling daily chores to be done quickly and without inconvenience. Always be very generous with the amount of working space in a birdroom because you will quickly find that you gather all manner of appliances—transport and show cages, feed bins, nest boxes, and so on. The more spacious the room, the easier it is to keep clean.

Among the fitments you should check out are light dimmers,

thermostats for heaters, ionizers for air purification, automatic watering systems (depending on the number of flights or cages to be serviced), possibly humidifiers and cooling devices, and the different types of lighting that are available these days. It is crucial that you feature good ventilation. A lack of this is a prime cause of the spread of disease.

Aviaries are a major investment for the parrot enthusiast, so they should be the subject of much research. Visit as many hobbyists as possible. This will bring rich rewards in the advice it yields, both from practical and esthetic viewpoints.

All aviary owners make mistakes, or think of better designs after they have completed their aviaries. They will be the first to advise you what they could have done to have made it better. You are almost certainly going to have to make some compromises, so the more advice you have that has stemmed from the experiences of others, the better you will be able to make sound judgments.

FEEDING PARROTS

The vast majority of parrot species are very easy to cater to in respect to their dietary needs. Apart from the foods you will no doubt have in your kitchen, your pet shop stocks a range of seeds, as well as commercially prepared mixes and treats that are fortified with extra vitamins and minerals.

The owner with just one or two parrots is advised to purchase ready mixed bags or cartons of large or small parrot mixes. This will probably be the most economic way to feed. The multi-owner or breeder should purchase seeds by weight and make up his own mix. This will save wasting money on seeds the birds largely ignore. However, when buying in bulk, do not go overboard to save a few dollars, risking the seed may go bad because you are not able to store it satisfactorily.

STORING SEED

Seeds must be kept in airtight containers or bins so they are protected from fouling by rodents and from flies and other insects alighting on them. Keep in a cool, dark cupboard, or place where they will not be subject to excessive heat or direct sunlight. It is essential that seed never gets damp, otherwise it will go sour and moldy within hours and become highly toxic.

In addition to a well balanced seed mixture, there are many fruits and vegetables that your parrot will enjoy. These can be fed raw, and should be thoroughly washed prior to feeding.

FOOD AND WATER CONTAINERS

You will need two food containers, plus one for grit, and one for water. One of the food vessels is for seed, the other for a fruit and vegetable salad. The seed container can be of the automatic dispenser style, of which there are countless models, or be an open crock pot. The former is better for the smaller parrots, but be sure its opening will allow for sunflower seeds, which can clog small dispensers. Always tap dispensers daily to ensure the seeds are falling into the tray.

Larger parrots will soon demolish plastic dispensers and therefore a heavy pot or strong metal seed dish is more feasible. When open pots are used, be sure to blow the husks every day, otherwise the pot may look full, but may only contain husks. Water should be changed daily to ensure freshness. Seed should always be available on an ad lib basis.

Grit is vital to birds because having no teeth they rely on this to help grind the seeds into a pulp in their stomach. You can purchase it from your local pet shop. Be sure to ask for a size suitable for the species you keep: small grit will not be satisfactory for the medium to larger parrots.

Parrots are notoriously wasteful feeders, especially with fruit, vegetables, bread and their like. With this in mind, it is better to provide small slices and prepare these as a salad. Take note of what is preferred and

Parrots are just like humans in that they will prefer one food over another. When feeding your parrot a mixture of foodstuffs, he will often search through to find his favorite first.

adjust the quantities of each item so waste is minimal. Do not withhold items just because they are not especially favored—they may be contributing a useful ingredient, albeit in trace amounts.

Parrots are just like us in that they have their moods in liking some foods but not others. Try to avoid letting your parrot get too

choosy by pandering only to its favored items. The pet should take a varied and balanced diet that includes a range of foods that will provide the carbohydrates, protein, and fats needed, as well as items (fruit, plants, vegetables) that are rich in vitamins.

There are numerous tonics and vitamin supplements you can purchase for the bird who refuses to take a wide range of foods. For those birds that do take a wide range of foods, tonics and vitamin supplements are not only cost wasteful, but can be dangerous. An excess of vitamins can upset the metabolic absorption of other vitamins and cause hypervitaminosis. Such supplements should only be given under veterinary advice because their accumulative use can be compared to giving medicines when they are not needed.

POPULAR SEEDS

A typical parrot mix will contain canary seed, various millets,

Fresh corn-on-the-cob is a well-liked treat by all parrots. This little budgie has his eyes set on this entire ear.

SOAKED SEEDS

When seeds are soaked in water for 24 hours this makes them softer and easier to digest. As such, they are especially beneficial to young birds, breeding hens, and those recovering from illness. If they are left to soak for a further 12-24 hours they will start to germinate. In this form their protein content will rise, making them very nutritious. However, do not over germinate because they may then become toxic. Both soaked and germinated seeds have only a short feed life. Remove and discard those uneaten after a few hours. Millet on the ear (sprays) are especially favored when soaked.

sunflower seeds in their three forms (striped, white, and black—the latter being the least liked), hemp, maw, and other seeds taken in small quantities, such a rape, niger, and teasel. Other cereal crops that may be given will include wheat, maize, and corn on the cob. Flaked cereals, as supplied to rabbits, will also be enjoyed by some parrots, but not by others. The seeds of all grasses will be enjoyed, as will those of many flowering plants. Nuts of all kinds will be taken with varying degrees of enthusiasm by larger parrots. Obviously, large, hard nuts cannot be cracked by the smaller species, so can be crushed by you in order that your pet can cope with them. Although a pinch of salt acts as a good tonic for all animals, do not feed salted peanuts to your parrot—give the unsalted peanut which is rich in protein and well liked. Pine nuts are especially enjoyed by the larger species.

By placing fresh fruits and vegetables in a fun arrangement for your parrot, he will not only benefit from their nutritious content but will have much fun in eating them.

FRUITS, VEGETABLES, AND PLANTS

Parrots are very cosmopolitan in the range of plant matter they will enjoy. Even the Australian parakeets, which are famed for their ability to survive well on an almost all seed diet, will benefit from a regular supply of plant matter. Do remember that most parrots come from regions rich in fruits and other plants, and therefore must have these within their day to day meals.

Apples, pears, strawberries, bananas, grapes, raisins, currants, berries, kiwis, melon, pineapple, figs, dates, elderberries, and blackberries are but a sampling of the fruits you can give your parrot. Carrots, beans, peas, celery, broccoli, soybean, mung beans, spinach, beets, cauliflower, and watercress are examples of the many vegetables that will be eaten

This Umbrella Cockatoo has a feast set in front of it. Fresh fruits and vegetables should be fed in small quantities, in addition to a balanced seed mixture, and not be the sole constituent.

The hard outer shells of walnuts are very easy for macaws and cockatoos to break open, however, smaller parrots will require you to break these open first.

with varying degrees of relish.

Among wild plants, dandelion, plantain, coltsfoot, parsley, chickweed, seeding grasses, sow thistle and garden flowering heads are again but a few offerings that will be selectively favored. Always ensure that all plant matter foods are rinsed to remove potential residual chemicals, and possibly fecal matter on gathered wild plants. Bunches of wild plants can be hung in the cage and aviary. Do not feed any plants grown from bulbs, nor any that may be poisonous; if you are unsure, do not supply the plant.

OTHER FOODS

Contrary to what is often thought, many parrots enjoy small amounts of cooked lamb or beef on the bone. They will spend much time nibbling at the hard bones. Mealworms (never maggots) and other small invertebrates will be taken by some birds, especially if the birds are breeding. Bread soaked in milk, butter, meat extracts, honey, and cheese are examples of protein rich foods that will be enjoyed according to individual taste. Pure fruit juices will be especially favored by some parrots.

With certain items you can make mash, including small seeds and just a drop of cod liver oil. Do not feed chocolate, candies and other sweet foods in excess. These should be fed sparingly. Should you purchase any of the nectar feeding birds, commercial nectar can be purchased conveniently from your local pet shop, which is the most convenient way of supplying this. Bear in mind that the nectar feeders still eat seeds and fruits in addition to the nectar.

Ensure that any extra treat foods are supplied in enough quantities for all birds that are housed together. Do not give the opportunity for an argument to occur.

PLANNING FEEDING REGIMENS

Your pet's diet should always be the source of both creativity and planning. When you first obtain the bird, ask what it has been feeding on. Maintain this diet during its first few settling in days. Next, start to offer additional items one at a time, so you can better gauge what the bird thinks of them. If you suddenly supply lots of new items it will select the favored ones and you will never really know if it would have acquired a taste for the others.

Make notes on those foods especially liked. These will be useful for tempting the pet to continue eating should it become ill. Never give a glut of any one food as this will cause stomach upsets.

In concluding this chapter a humorous remark, but one which has an excellent philosophy, is worth quoting. The famed English parrot owner, the late Duke of Bedford, had given a lecture on feeding parrots. Afterwards, a lady approached him and stated that her parrot had only been given seeds and was still living after 20 years on this diet. His reply is said to have been, "Madam, your parrot is not living, it's just taking a long while to die!"

Always feed a varied diet, and be prepared to experiment in a common sense manner and your pet will enjoy peak health, wonderful plumage, and will always look forward to its next meal.

TRAINING YOUR PARROT

Parrots are among the most intelligent of all birds. This means they can be very good, terribly naughty, highly mischievous, and extremely confiding. They are capable of learning many tricks, and of course, some are super mimics. You do not need to purchase a costly bird in order to enjoy these attributes. The tiny budgerigar, often overlooked by many potential owners, is one of the most capable of parrots, while to this and most other parrot owners and writers, the cockatiel is the supreme parrot when viewed on a "more for your money" basis.

In this short chapter, discussion is directed at enabling you to develop a strong bond of trust with your pet. Only when this is achieved can you progress to other things. For most owners, simply having a really friendly parrot is all they want. It must be stressed from the outset that a parrot confined to its cage for long periods will never make a wonderful pet. To create a bond with any animal requires that it be handled, touched, and allowed to feel free and involved with its owner and other family members.

FEATHER TRIMMING

Whether or not you prefer to trim the flight feathers of your parrot in order to make training easier is a matter of personal preference. This author does not, but you should make your decision based on the following, and on which you would feel happier and more confident about. Of course, if you have purchased a hand-reared baby you will already have passed this stage, so the comments will apply only for your ongoing situation.

Advantages of Trimming

When the primary feathers of each wing are trimmed your parrot cannot gain altitude. It is more willing to alight on your hand as a place of safety than if it has the freedom to fly around the room. Left to free-fly, it is less likely to let you approach it, and it can also injure itself more easily if it can fly because it may crash into windows. Should it escape your home, it will fly away in panic and probably get lost.

Advantages of Not Trimming

Your pet is being left as nature intended it. More patience is needed in taming; from this develops a strong bond because the training progresses at the bird's pace rather than one forced upon it by its physical handicap. Should the bird escape your home its natural defense—the ability to fly—may well save its life from cats, dogs, or other dangers.

If you decide to trim the feathers do not think this is permanent. The feathers will be replaced at each molt (once or twice a year). You thus have the option to trim initially, then let things return to normal at the next molt. By that time your pet will be very tame. In order that the feathers do not look unsightly after trimming, leave the outermost primary. If you wish to let the bird have some flight ability, trim every alternative feather of the ten primaries—this way you will not even notice the feathers have been trimmed.

CAGE TAMING

If you decide to leave the feathers intact it is better to tame the bird while it is in its cage. Once it is confident in your hand being in its own domain, it will not be frightened at stepping onto this when it is permitted room freedom. Further, should it escape into a nearby tree, it will be more familiar with flying onto your hand or

The door of your parrot's cage should be large enough so that you can remove the bird from this and have plenty of room around him.

shoulder, so there will be a better chance (not guaranteed) that it will come to you.

You can start cage training the day after you have obtained the bird and it has had time to settle, view its surroundings, and have a night's sleep. It is best to work with your pet in the evening when it is less active. There must be no distractions at all, and do it when

no one else is in the room. Offer the parrot tidbits and talk in a soft voice. You will need to sit near the cage for quite some time, and the pet will be watching your every move. At first it will snatch the tidbit and retreat from your hand, but slowly it will gain confidence and stay put. When this stage is reached, place your hand such that the pet must come towards you to get the treat.

It is very important to take this first step slowly. Your objective is to reach that point where your pet will sit and eat its treat while your hand moves around in front of it. If it is startled, it will retreat to the cage bars, but just leave your hand resting on the perch and let it come back to you to get the treat. Soon it will sit quite happily near your hand, and this is when you can proceed to the next crucial stage. Place your index finger just above its legs, near its lower chest. It will either retreat, lower its head and nip your finger, or step onto this. When taming any animal there is always that point when a degree of risk is involved, this is why the first stage is so crucial in order to minimize the risk of a fear bite. Watch the parrot's eyes when your hand approaches it. If they are dilating rapidly, this indicates fear and possible aggression—go back to the first stage for a little longer.

Remember, a parrot may "test" your finger to see if it's a suitable perch—this is not aggression. Ultimately, it will simply hook or press its upper mandible on your finger to provide a momentary brace while it moves its foot to the finger. It may alight without using its beak, depending on where you

allowed out of its cage. This is best done in a small room where there is less chance of it knocking things over, and where it cannot gain too much speed, thus risk hurting itself in collision with a wall or window. Draw the curtains or windows to remove this latter risk. It will always seek the highest vantage point.

This first out of cage experience should be permitted only when you have ample time to stay with your pet so you can supervise things. Do not allow other pets

Once you have tamed your parrot it will be safe to allow him to accompany you wherever you go. Be sure there is no chance that your parrot can escape while on outdoor excursions.

have placed the finger in relation to its feet. Parrots never step down, only up, so always be sure your finger is placed so this is possible. When moving down it will always use its beak as a brace or "hand." The benefit of having a large cage, and those that have platform facility, will become self evident when hand taming a parrot. Once your pet is very confident in your hand it can be

into the room at this stage. Let the bird have ample time to fly around and explore this new territory. It will not be too keen to return to its cage after having been confined to one for maybe quite a number of weeks at the dealer's store.

However, when it starts to get hungry, it will go to its cage. Alternatively, you must take it there. It may fly from your finger a few times but, with patience, and maybe a treat in its it claws, it will let you place it back to the cage which is a secure retreat for it. Hereafter, if it is allowed ample time out of the cage, it will invariably go to the cage itself when it is hungry or tired. The cage has then truly become its home rather than a prison.

HANDLING YOUR PET

Finger taming is but the first stage of bonding with a parrot. Once it is happy on your hand you can sit down and it will then want to climb up your arm to your shoulder, and maybe even onto your head. It will "test" your neck and

A parrot will "test" your finger for its firmness. This is not an act of aggression, only a way for it to tell if your hand is sturdy enough for it to walk on.

hair, probably your ear as well, so be aware of this. As it gets more confident in you, it will allow you to stroke its cheeks and neck—this being very pleasurable to the bird. Approach these aspects with the same patience you did with hand taming. It is a slow but steady series of progressions.

The ultimate is when it will let you stroke its wings and allow you to lift it bodily. This requires

the parrot having great confidence in you. By this stage you will even be able to start flipping it on its back and playing with it. You have achieved the perfect bond with your parrot, and it will by now be the love and pride of your life!

You must appreciate that to achieve this level of companionship with a bird that was not hand tamed as a youngster is infinitely more difficult than if you had paid the extra cash to buy such a bird in the first place.

FEAR OF BEING BITTEN

If you are fearful of being bitten by a medium to larger parrot the answer is not to buy one in the first place. Many owners fail to take this advice. The result is the pet is relegated to becoming a sad, caged pet for the rest of its life. You can use a short wooden perch to help in initial taming, but sooner or later you will have to let the parrot alight onto your finger. Do not use gloves because you lose the sensation of touch.

If you do purchase a medium

There are many dangers in the home that you should be cautious of while your pet parrot is out. Open fish tanks and pots cooking on the stove are two of the most common ways pet parrots are injured.

precautions to protect your pet from potential injury when it is free to roam about. Unless you have a small, spare room where the parrot can be allowed to play while you are out, it is best to restrict it to its cage during such periods, and give it lots of out of cage time when you are present. Sources of danger for the pet are open fires, and those with no protective mesh in front of them, chimneys, extractor fans, toxic indoor plants, open fish tanks, trailing electric wires that are plugged into a socket, open windows, open doors when there could be a through draft causing them to slam, and tons of dangerous chemicals, such as insecticides, paints, aerosols, and their like.

Additionally, it is wise to remove fragile ornaments that might be knocked from shelves by your pet as it clambers or flies around the room. Never allow the parrot into the kitchen. Not only does this room hold many dangers for the pet, but it is a prudent health precaution.

sized parrot, and subsequently develop a fear of it biting you because it was not tame, please do not relegate it to being a caged bird. Sell it and purchase a smaller species, or one that was hand reared. This may prove to be the ideal parrot for your particular needs.

PRECAUTIONS IN THE HOME

Once you become a parrot owner you must take due

BREEDING

Within the confines of a single short chapter, it is obviously not possible to discuss in any detail the breeding needs of the numerous individual species. The discussion is therefore a basic primer that will apply to the breeding of all parrots. If you decide to proceed you are advised to seek works devoted to the species you have obtained, and which will give you the extra information needed.

GENERAL ADVICE

If you are a first time parrot owner and wish to become a breeder, you are strongly advised not to commence

It is not easy to breed birds, especially parrots. Chicks are very fragile and should the parents not care for it properly, owner intervention may be the only way to save such a bird.

with any but the commonly available species that have long established captive breeding records. These are budgerigars, cockatiels, lovebirds, or possibly one or two of the smaller Australian parakeets or South American conures.

By taking this route your chances of success will be considerably greater, and problems fewer. The experience and contacts you gain along the way can then be applied to more ambitious programs in which the more difficult species are tackled. If you attempt to commence with birds that require more knowledge than you have, frustration and disappointment are likely. You will then give up and leave the hobby because you attempted to run before you could walk.

BEFORE STARTING

All too often beginners rush into things, as in buying pets, accommodations, or breeding. Things will go a lot smoother if you plan for breeding

attempts. You will need extra space for cages to stock the youngsters once they are weaned. You will need bins for the extra seed, as well as more feeding utensils. Although many parrots will breed readily in cages, you should have one or two aviaries in which non-breeding birds can be given ample exercise in order to bring them into breeding condition. At the very least you will need good sized indoor flights to provide this.

You will also need record books so that the results of your breedings can be logged. Such records will be important in helping you develop a history of your stock—and for planning future matings. The records will indicate the birds that were paired, their colors (if appropriate), their age, and their ring numbers, or other marks of identification.

The incubation time must be noted, together with number of eggs, how many hatched, color of youngsters, their sexes if these can be ascertained, how many survived to fledging time, when this was, and the diet given. If you are breeding species in which

Large macaws need large nesting sites that can withstand the strength of their beaks. Many nesting sites for macaws are reinforced with metal to ensure that they do not chew through.

mutations are involved, always try to record what is known of the genotype.

OBTAINING BREEDING STOCK

If you have taken earlier advice, and are beginning with well proven breeding species, you will have no problems obtaining breeding stock. This is best purchased from a reputable breeder who can be contacted either via a show, or by writing to

the national association for that species. Your local pet shop may also have a regular customer that they can refer you to.

If you plan to commence with lesser established, or the larger, parrots, you should be aware of your immediate problems. When birds are advertised as pairs, this does not always mean one of each sex, it simply means two birds. In the non dimorphic species, which includes most of the medium to larger parrots, you must obtain a sexed pair. This means their sex will have been established either by endoscopic examination of their reproductive organs, or by DNA testing from toenail or other blood samples.

Even when you have obtained a true pair you may not know how old they are and, more important, they may not be compatible. Even with compatible birds they may not settle down to breed for months, even years! You would ideally need to obtain a proven breeding pair. These will be very costly, and it does not always follow that because they bred for the previous owner they will do so for you. They may also have passed their best breeding age, which may be the reason they are being sold. One way or another, it makes more sense to start with species that will give you success. So, the breeder of a popular species will select a pair of young birds for you, whose age can be verified either from the leg bands or from the breeder's records. Do not start with too many pairs, perhaps two to four would be best. Obtain these from two or more different breeders so you have flexibility in your initial breeding lines. Do not mix and match these pairs if they are from carefully bred lines. Keep them as original lines, and only start to cross them if this is needed.

If you are happy with the outcome of your first breedings, go back to the original breeder for extra stock from that line. This is sound breeding strategy, a subject you are advised to study via books on genetics.

BREEDING CONDITION

Never breed a bird that is not in the peak of fitness, especially the hen. A male's initial contribution is purely its sperms, but the hen has an ongoing relationship with the embryos. If she is unfit or obese this will effect the health and vigor of the eggs and chicks. Aviary exercise is by far the best way to bring pairs into breeding condition. If one of the pair is recovering from an illness, delay breeding that pair.

BREEDING SEASON

The best time to breed your birds is during the spring through summer months, when the days are longer and warmer, and when fresh greenfoods are most plentiful. The popular parrots can be bred year 'round, but this means having artificial lighting to create a 12 hour light/dark cycle, and the provision of a sound heating system. Gain experience before you attempt winter breedings.

This is a typical nest box for budgerigars, lovebirds, and some species of grass parakeets. Larger parrot species will take the same basic design, however, the dimensions will be much larger.

NEST BOXES

All parrots utilize a wooden nest box in which to lay eggs and rear the chicks. Very few build nests, the majority lay the eggs on a floor covering of shavings, twigs, feathers and similar materials crudely fashioned to retain the eggs. In the wild they lay in the rotted trunks and boughs of dead or dying trees.

Your can purchase nest boxes from your pet shop or make your own suited to the species you keep. If the birds are being bred in an aviary and the nest box is outside, even if it is under a canopy, the box must be of stout construction so that it can withstand heat and cold, thus maintain a constant internal temperature. The thickness of the wood should be a minimum of 34in (19mm).

In design, the favored style is one that is taller than it is wide or deep. There should be a sloping and overhanging roof to take water away if the nest box is unprotected. An entrance hole and landing perch should be placed to one side of center on the front face. The hole should be just large enough for the hen to enter— if she wants it larger she will attend to this herself.

On the same face, but inside, it is best to nail struts of wood to form a ladder. These are superior to weldwire, in which hens and chicks can get their toes entangled. At the base of the box place a concave of stout wood. This keeps the eggs in the center for better brooding, and stops the hen from whittling at the nest box base.

Just above the concave height, on a side wall or the rear, there should be an inspection door. It is better at this location than in the top. You can more readily collect or inspect the eggs or chicks when necessary. If your hens become familiar with nest inspection it will not be resented, and will enable you to supplement the feeding of chicks that are lagging behind other siblings. You can also make regular weight checks to see that the chicks are steadily gaining.

The dimensions of the nest box will normally be such that the width and depth are a little larger than the beak to rump length of the hen—forget the tail in the longtailed species. The height will be two to five times the width, depending on the species.

The smaller parrot species lay more eggs and hatch more chicks in one clutch than the larger species. Some larger species such as the cockatoo and macaw only lay 1-3 eggs at a time, and rarely hatch and raise all of these to fledgling age.

The nesting site of large macaws should be located as high as possible within their enclosure to closely simulate their wild environment.

Budgerigars, cockatiels, and lovebirds cope quite well in relatively small boxes with respect to the height dimension.

SITING THE NEST BOX

If in an aviary, place the nest box high up and shaded from direct sunlight. It is often wise to place two or more nest boxes so the pair has a choice. Those not used can be taken down once a selection has been made. If a pair fails to commence breeding after due time, it may be because the nest box site is not to their liking. Try another spot, as this often results in success.

Some breeders leave nest boxes up year 'round, and the birds use these for roosting in. Others prefer to take them down at the end of the season so that late or early clutches are not produced. It is important that nest boxes are assembled using screws. This allows you to take them apart each season and thoroughly disinfect them with bleach. Failure to do this can result in mites and other parasitic invasions of the parents and the chicks.

BREED IN PAIRS

Although some parrots, including budgies and cockatiels, will readily breed on a colony system, this is not advised for a number of reasons.

1. Some pairs may prove very belligerent to others, invading their nests and killing the chicks.
2. Fighting is likely between pairs as they seek to obtain the nest box they feel is the best—even when these are all more or less in line on the same side of the aviary.
3. You have no control over which birds pair with which. In popular species you will invariably want to have such control in order to obtain the colors desired.

EGG LAYING AND REARING

If all has gone well, and the pair has mated, the hen will lay her eggs and appropriately incubate them for the specific time for her species. In some species the cocks will help incubate and feed the

Breeding pairs of parrots develop a very close relationship and frequently display moments of true affection and devotion.

young, in others they only feed the hen, and maybe the babies once these start to leave the nest.

Many things can go wrong during egg laying and incubation—eggbinding being a not uncommon happening. This is created by a number of causes. Common reasons are because the hen lacked calcium in her diet, the weather is cold, or the hen is obese, or out of condition. An eggbound hen will be seen to leave the nest and perch in a distressed state—she may even be unable to stay on the perch.

You must act promptly with such a bird and place it in a warm cage. The temperature should be about 90°F (32°C), at which the hen should be able to pass the problem egg within a few hours. If she clearly remains distressed, your vet must be contacted otherwise it is probable the hen will die from straining.

Eggs can also be double shelled. In this case the chick is often unable to break out of its shell. In other instances an egg can become dehydrated, so the chick dies or, if the humidity level is too high, the chick will drown in the shell. You should endeavor to minimize these possibilities by avoiding the conditions in the first place.

Even before the chicks leave the nest, the hen may lay a second round of eggs. This is when the cock will start to feed the first round fledglings. Once they are eating independently they should be moved to nursery cages. Seed should be sprinkled on the cage floor until you are sure they know where the seed pots are. Likewise, water can be given in open pots as well as dispensers. Perches in nursery cages should be lower than normal. Never sell youngsters unless you are very sure they are eating independently. Throughout the breeding period it is very important that breeding birds have an excellent diet. The addition of a calcium supplement is beneficial in helping to avoid eggbinding.

The hand rearing of parrots is a complex and time intensive process, so beginners should not undertake this unless it is forced upon them due to the loss of the hen. Both this aspect, and the fostering, or artificial incubation of eggs, is now quite a standard

African Grey babies only a few days old. Parrots must be banded with closed rings when only a few days old for identification purposes.

Some birds will allow the owner to peek in the nest and inspect the chicks. It is not advised to do this too often, however, because the parents may become too upset and may abandon the chicks. This is a nest of three-week-old lovebirds.

procedure in some species. You should invest in a good book devoted to this aspect before contemplating these more skilled operations.

IDENTIFICATION

Your options for identification are between split leg bands and water based paint marks (temporary), or underwing tattooing, microchip implant, or closed, dated and numbered leg bands (permanent). The smaller species, such as budgerigars and cockatiels, normally have closed, metal leg bands, which are often obligatory on exhibition birds. Larger species will often be tattooed, or have microchip implants, though this latter method is much more costly. Split bands can be placed on a parrot of any age. They may be colored or striped. However, all but the smallest parrots can usually remove these without difficulty. Closed metal bands are placed onto the chicks when they are just a few days old. It is essential that the correct size ring is obtained for your species otherwise problems will arise if it proves too tight. The breeding of any parrot species is a highly rewarding part of the hobby, but it should be undertaken only after considerable thought, and then only if you are sure you have the needed time to devote to the parents and their chicks.

EXHIBITING PARROTS

For many breeders, exhibition is the logical conclusion to their program in that it gives them the opportunity to have their stock assessed in a competitive framework. To others, who have not bred the parrots they own, it is an opportunity to display their skill in having been able to bring the bird into superb physical condition.

For the potential parrot owner the bird show is a place where many species can be seen in one location. The parrot exhibition is thus a one stop venue where all involved in the parrot hobby can converge for different reasons. At the larger shows there will be many booths selling parrot equipment, seeds, and even birds, so all hobbyists are recommended to visit these entertaining spectacles.

TYPES OF SHOW

The most numerous parrot exhibitions, and the largest for any single species, will be those devoted exclusively to the budgerigar. The cockatiel and the lovebirds come next in size of specialty shows, with some of the other popular species being seen in group shows, such as those devoted to Australian parrots and so on. There are then the all parrot shows in which many species can be seen.

National avicultural exhibitions will feature all cage and aviary birds. At these, the parrots are usually well represented. At local levels, both parrot societies and foreign bird clubs will hold small shows in which a range of cage birds are to be seen. There are thus a number of types of shows that you can attend, and are

This is a typical scene at a bird exhibition. After all judging has taken place, the public is permitted to walk around and view the winners.

All birds, especially parrots, show themselves off better at a show in a cage against a light colored background.

advertised both locally and in national avicultural magazines.

EXHIBITION JUDGING AND CLASSES

Parrots are judged either against a written standard of excellence, as in budgerigars, or based on their physical condition (the quality of their plumage and general appearance). Most parrots are subject to judgment upon their physical condition.

In budgerigars, cockatiels, and lovebirds, there are classes for each of the color mutations, as well as for the two sexes. The winning birds from each color group go forward to meet those of other groups until a Best in Show winner is declared.

Exhibitors are graded based on their success—so there are novice, intermediate, and champion exhibitors. Parrot shows will also feature classes in which pairs of the same species are assessed either as true pairs, or as a pair that is comparable in their quality—depending on whether the species exhibits dimorphism.

Nearly all shows involving psittacines will of course have classes for talking birds. In these, quality and extent of vocabulary are the characterstics that the judges look for.

THE EXHIBITION PARROT

Before a parrot can be exhibited it must be carefully prepared so that it is in super condition with immaculate plumage. This is an ongoing discipline for the exhibitor, who must ensure only the best of nutrition is given to the birds, and the best of general care. The parrot must also be well trained so it will show itself to good effect—not being frightened by the show, and crouching in a corner such that it cannot be fairly judged. Very many hours go into training a top budgerigar or other parrot.

Other than in pet or talking classes, a parrot's owner must be a member of a local club to compete in their member shows, or be a member of a national society to enter into the large open shows. An open show simply means it is open to all owners who are not members of the club sponsoring the show, though they will be members of one or more other clubs.

SHOW CAGES

The very popular show birds, such as budgerigars, must be exhibited in a cage that meets the exact requirements of their national society. The larger parrots are not subject to this requirement and are exhibited in whatever cage their owners keep them in.

Becoming an Exhibitor

The best way to become an exhibitor is to join either your local foreign bird society, or your national species club, or parrot society. At their local meetings you will learn everything you need to know to become an exhibitor, and whether your birds are considered good enough for competition. Do understand that exhibiting these birds is very time and cost consuming. Consider such things as getting to the shows, entry fees, and training your birds.

However, you can restrict your involvement to just the local shows, so you can dial in the sort of time and cost suited to your pocket. Many find that the exhibition becomes the focus of all of their spare time—such is the magnetic effect it can have.

A wonderful display of the winning budgies at a show. Note the array of prize winning ribbons and typical stock show cage each budgie is housed in.

MAINTAINING GOOD HEALTH

The key to maintaining good health in a parrot lies within its nutrition, high standards of hygiene, and the owner's ability to notice changes in the appearance or behavior of his/her pet and to react quickly to this. If these matters are attended to it is most unlikely the bird will ever suffer any but the most minor of complaints. The owner with just one or two parrots is largely insulated from many of the problems that can befall the breeder.

It would be easy to catalog the diseases of birds, together with their treatments, but this approach is hardly of practical use to the majority of owners, who are neither able to diagnose disease, nor qualified to understand the full effect of treatments. The approach therefore taken in this chapter is to highlight areas of husbandry where the problems invariably begin.

The novice owner should ensure that his strategy will avoid these situations. The more advanced hobbyist should make an honest assessment of his husbandry techniques to see if these are not in need of improvement when compared with the situation he started out with some years earlier.

For those that have many parrots, the risk born out of the numbers kept will greatly increase the potential for problems. These invariably arise through any of the following causes:

1. **Lack of hygiene.** Many breeders build up their stock more rapidly than they have the time to devote to them. Cleaning becomes more hurried, or neglected, and this paves the way for colonization by pathogens.
   Remedy: If you recognize this as a reality, start to reduce stock to that number you can cope with in the time you have available.

2. **Cages and equipment are in poor state of repair.** Cages which have worn perches, rusting weldwire, cracked feeder pots, and floors stained from the liquid content of fecal matter are not easily maintained. They take more time to clean, yet still remain a haven for mites, lice, and all manner of bacteria.
   Remedy: Renew caging that has long past its practical purpose. Replace with modern cages that are readily disinfected. Always have spare perches and feeders so old ones can be replaced by rotation on a regular basis. Carefully clean and paint cage bars and weldwire.

3. **Overcrowding.** It is difficult to determine exactly when a breeding room is overcrowded. When it is stocked such that

there is insufficient space for all appliances to be stored neatly and no ample working space exists, you are well on the road to this state. When birds are having to share cages that you would preferably not have them share, you have reached an overcrowded state. When you are stacking cages in every possible place in order to increase your stock numbers, you are overcrowding.

Remedy: Establish the number of birds you feel is adequate for a given stock or breeding room, then do not go over this limit. Erect a second separate stockroom, or thin down your stock if you find you have gone way past your original number.

4. **Lack of ventilation and environmental control.** When combined with the other conditions already discussed, a lack of ventilation will prove devastating. On its own, in a well planned birdroom, it will be the major precursor of illness. Unless fresh air (not drafts) can remove stale air, the bacteria that is in the stale air will merely increase in numbers. Remember also that pathogens are held in tiny droplets of water in the air. If very humid conditions are suddenly "dried," the water will evaporate and the pathogens in them will be released.

Sudden fluctuations in temperature will also create havoc in a birdroom, because

Good hygiene is important to the health of your stock. This fight cage is in dire need of basic care, the perches need to be cleaned or replaced and some of the wood towards the back should be cared for as well.

Overcrowding is another way that birds quickly fall ill. Be sure to only house an amount that will be comfortable together and will not cause the birds stress.

they will create stress in the birds. In this state they are much more easily attacked by disease organisms.

Remedy: Be sure your stockroom is ventilated both at a low and high level at opposite ends of the room so as to encourage through ventilation. Try to maintain a constant temperature, as well as controlled light/dark cycles. Manual on/off light and heat switches are notoriously poor controllers. Fit rheostats and thermostats to control these important environmental factors. The use of ionizers in breeding rooms is recommended in order to keep dust and bacteria levels to a minimum.

5. **No quarantine facility.** A breeder with no quarantine facility is asking for a disaster. The facility does not need to be elaborate or costly, the main aspect being that it is a cage or indoor flight not in the same building as the main stock. It must be very clean and well disinfected after each use. All newly acquired birds should be kept in this isolation unit for about 21 days, giving time for any incubating illness to show itself. At the same time, the bird(s) can be routinely wormed and treated for external parasites with

preparations from your vet. The diet can be observed. By this approach you can be reasonably satisfied that by the time the bird joins your main stock it will not be taking any major problems with it. If you exhibit birds, it would be prudent to keep your exhibition team separate from your main breeding stock. In this way you dramatically minimize the possibility that a team member will transport any problems back from the show to infect the rest of your stock.

Remedy: Incorporate a quarantine facility.

6. **Lack of hospital cage facility.** It is a fact of life that many breeders do not prepare for problems, working on the assumption they will never get them. The very minimum that any parrot owner should have in the way of useful appliances is a dull emitter infrared lamp. This is best wired through a thermostat that will control the upper limit temperature. A homemade hospital cage should be large enough that the patient can move towards or away from the heat source to satisfy its own comfort. Thermometers at either end of the cage and protected from

Only those parrot species that are compatible should be housed together. Be very careful of placing larger species in with smaller ones because they can do accidental damage just from the obvious size difference.

Larger parrot species should be housed in equal pairs otherwise fights may break out and serious damage to your stock may occur.

the bird's beak, are useful in double checking that the thermostat is working correctly. Such a cage should be made so that it can be cleaned very easily. A low, as well as normal height, perch should be included. The heat source should be at one end, either above the cage, at the end, or at the front. The desired temperature is 85-90°F(29-32°C). Heat alone really can work wonders for an ailing bird, and should be the first action taken when this is suspected. Commercial hospital cages are available, but rather costly, especially if they are large enough to house the medium to larger parrots. They may also stress some birds, which can be counter productive.

Remedy: Do not wait until you have a problem. A heated cage facility should be regarded as obligatory to any breeder, while an infrared lamp is a non costly appliance for the pet owner.

7. **Lack of prompt action.** It is important that if a parrot is suspected of being unwell it be removed away from all other birds and pets as soon as possible. Do not wait for another 24 hours to see how things progress. If there is a disease, you have given it the extra time to infect other birds.

8. **Not recognizing health problems.** In many instances a parrot may not display clinical signs of an illness. The best you may get is a change in the parrot's behavior. To appreciate this you must know each bird as an individual. This can be difficult if large numbers of birds are kept. Nonetheless it must be attempted by spending time observing the stock. The signs you are looking for are: the bird shows little interest in its food or water; it shows little interest in what is going on around it; it seeks a quiet spot away from other birds; it sits hunched on its perch with both feet grasping this; its head is lowered, rather than being rested between its wings when sleeping; it is scratching itself more than any normal bird would.

Any of these behaviors should

Feather plucking is a destructive habit that parrots sometimes resort to because of boredom, poor diet conditions, or lack of stimulation. Once a bird reaches this sad state it is often difficult to get it to stop.

see you isolating the bird, noting the reasons you have observed, and inspecting the bird more closely for any initial clinical signs. Now contact your vet and relate your observations. Keep a careful watch on all other birds.

9. **Attempting home diagnosis.** Many owners and breeders will contribute to their own problems by attempting home diagnosis. In this day and age veterinarians have far more knowledge of avian diseases, and worthwhile treatments, than in the past. Clinical signs of illness are often similar for a range of problems, so the only way specific pathogens can be isolated is by microscopy of blood or fecal samples. An incorrect diagnosis will result in lost time. Ineffective old remedies may result in a dead parrot.

Even with the advanced diagnostic equipment and drugs available these days, it has to be said that there remains an element of chance in treatments, but your vet is better educated to make judgments than you are.

AUTOPSY

The breeder is wisely counseled to always have an autopsy on a parrot that dies suddenly and for no apparent reason. If the cause can be identified it may save other valuable birds from the same fate. Place the body in a suitable plastic box and keep it refrigerated (not frozen) if you cannot take it straight to the vet.

THE AFTERMATH OF PROBLEMS

Whenever an illness has appeared in one or more parrots the wise owner will immediately review all husbandry techniques. If the problem has been parasitic, it is essential that thorough cleaning and repeat treatments of accommodations are effected to eradicate eggs that were not destroyed at the initial treatment. All perches and branches are best destroyed if the problem was serious. Likewise, nest boxes that are at all questionable as to their state of repair should be destroyed.

It is never possible to eliminate the risk of illness if you keep one or more parrots. The object of your management strategy is to minimize the possibility of it happening in the first place, then to contain it by prompt and aftermath actions, should it arise. Never assume "it could not happen to me" because that represents an over opportunistic attitude that will surely get you into trouble sooner or later. Prepare for the worst, and the chances are greater it will not happen. Concentrate all your efforts into preventative medicine, then build up your knowledge of avian diseases and conditions by reading about them rather than by practical experience of them.

Whenever an illness has affected one bird of your stock, it is wise to carefully examine all your other birds so that an epidemic does not break out.

The overall and general good health of your bird will show in its appearance. Tight feather condition as well as sparkling eyes and an overall active personality are signs of good health.

POPULAR PARROTS

It has been stressed in this book that the first time or novice parrot owner should restrict his choice of species to those that are well established in cages or aviaries, rather than purchase birds that may well prove to be difficult to maintain, exorbitantly costly to purchase, or very rarely offered for sale. This advice is reflected in the species discussed in this final chapter. In some instances the species are discussed individually, in others they are treated as a group of related species.

A PARROT'S SCIENTIFIC NAME

A basic understanding of parrot classification will be very helpful to you when seeking a particular species. While all popular parrots have common names (indeed may have a number of these), they will have only one scientific name that is unique to them, and is totally international in its usage. The latter is not so for common names, which is why you should be familiar with the scientific name of your parrot.

The scientific name is always a binomial, thus composed of two parts. The first part, the generic, denotes the genus the species is in. The second part, the specific or trivial, identifies the individual species in the genus. Only when the two names are used together do they uniquely identify a species. A subspecies is denoted by the use of a trinomial.

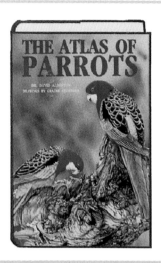

Atlas of Parrots of the World by Dr. D. Alderton. Contains illustrated coverage of every species and subspecies of parrot in the world. Hard cover, 544 pages, with over 300 full color plates.

Parrots of the World by J.M. Forshaw. This extraordinary work contains almost 500 species and subspecies with accounts of their habits in the wild. Hard cover, 584 pages and over 300 color plates.

The scientific name is always written in a typeface that differs from that of the main body of text, thus it invariably appears in italics. The genus always commences with a capital letter, the species name always with a lowercase.

BUDGERIGAR—*MELOPSITTACUS UNDULATUS* 18CM (7IN)

This tiny little parrot can be said to be the father of the parrot hobby. It is by far the most popular psittacine in the world; its numbers running into millions worldwide. It is an extremely lively, amusing, and chirpy pet. Being small, it will not offend neighbors with its call, nor will it reduce your furniture to firewood. Male budgies can become extremely accomplished talkers, and as exhibition birds they are without peer as far as color mutations go. No other bird is seen in as many color varieties.

Although quality breeding and show birds still command quite high prices, the average nice looking pet is the least expensive parrot you could own. If breeding is the objective, this little gem should definitely be on your short list. Its start-up costs will be lower than for any other species. Sexing is best done during the breeding season when the cere of the male becomes a purple-blue, that of the hen being brown. Immatures display barring on their heads, their throat spots are less obvious, and the white iris ring is absent, making the eye look larger. Adult plumage is acquired when about 3-4 months old. Longevity may exceed 10 years.

COCKATIEL—*NYMPHICUS HOLLANDICUS* 33CM (13IN)

If you feel the budgerigar is too small for you, the cockatiel may be the ideal first parrot to own. This author rates this bird as the supreme parrot for the beginner. It is also one of the finest choices for those wishing to breed or exhibit birds of this family. It is so good that finding any faults with it is all but impossible.

With its sprightly yellow crest, orange cheek spots, and gray, black, and white plumage, the cockatiel's nearest relatives are the much larger cockatoos. Unlike these, the male cockatiel has a pleasant whistling call note that is in no way offensive to the ear. Cockatiels, like budgies, have very docile temperaments and can be included in a mixed aviary with much smaller birds, including finches.

The little budgerigar is often referred to as the father of the parrot hobby. They are still the most popular of all parrot species and are well established in almost all countries.

The cockatiel makes a very wonderful pet that proves to be perfect for those who want something a little bigger than a budgie, yet not quite as large as some of the other parrot species.

As pets, they are truly delightful and affectionate parrots if obtained when young. Even the older cocky will become very tame if handled with care and patience. There are many mutations available. The lutino (yellow), albino, and the pied are but three stunningly beautiful varieties. The hen is a duller version of the male, and the underside of her tail is barred in black and yellow, as compared to the black and gray of the male. Juveniles are similar to the female. Adult plumage is attained when over six months old, and longevity may exceed 25 years.

This species will be more costly than a budgerigar, but really is worth the extra price for the bigger size and delightful temperament. These are strong flying birds so, if an aviary is to be their home, it should have as long a flight as possible. Like the budgerigar, cockatiels can be readily bred on a colony system, but pairs are suggested unless the colony is of one color variety.

THE LOVEBIRDS—GENUS *AGAPORNIS* 15CM (5.9IN)

The common name of these very robust little African parrots is misleading—at least when applied to their interactions with other birds, including those of their own species. The lovebirds can be extremely aggressive to birds of their own size or smaller, so they are not ideal for mixed aviaries. A bonded pair, however, will huddle together and be very

Cockatiels are available in a wide variety of colors. Pictured here is a beautiful lutino.

affectionate—for which they are named.

There are nine species of lovebirds, but only three can be regarded as readily available. As a group, they are all tough little parrots with short tails and quite large beaks for their size. They make delightful pets, and are very popular breeding and exhibition birds. There are a number of mutational forms, especially in the Peach-faced species. These birds are best obtained as babies because they are less readily tamed as they mature.

Being small, they are not as costly to cater for in respect of aviary or flight cage size. Sexing is

The smart little lovebird has been developed in a great number of mutational varieties. They are hardy, inexpensive to cater for, and prove to be quite comical.

difficult in the popular species because both look alike. The basic coloration within the group is green, with yellow, red, black, and blue being seen according to species. Adult plumage is attained when about four or more months of age, and longevity may exceed ten years. Keep these birds in pairs, either as pets or breeding birds. Cost is variable, but in their wild plumage color they are not expensive. They come well recommended as being playful, inquisitive, and easy to cater for. The three popular species are: Peach-faced lovebird, *A. roseicollis,* Masked lovebird, *A. personata,* and Fischer's lovebird, *A. fischeri.* The first is the slightly larger of the three.

Less readily seen, but available, are: Abyssinian or Black-winged, *A. taranta,* Gray-headed or Madagascar lovebird, *A. cana,* and the Red-faced lovebird, *A. pullaria.* Each of these are dimorphic, so can be sexed by visual appearance. The Nyasa lovebird, *A. lilianae,* is now quite scarce, and the sexes are similar. The other available species is the Black-cheeked lovebird, *A. nigrigenis,* in which the sexes are also similar. This is the smallest of the group.

AFRICAN GREY PARROT—*PSITTACUS ERITHACUS* 33CM (13IN)

This all grey, black beaked parrot is possibly the most well-known, and certainly the longest established, of the popular pet parrots. Expensive to purchase, being on par with the best of Amazon species, it makes an extremely devoted companion,

Lovebirds, as well as the majority of larger parrot species, enjoy natural wood branches within their cage both to walk on and to whittle.

The African Grey Parrot is well-known for its talking ability. Purchasing a parrot purely for its talking potential is unfair to the bird, and can be sadly disappointing for you.

Many household plants are toxic to your parrot. Be sure to supervise your pet at all times while he is away from his cage and do not even let him near any plants that may be toxic.

and is arguably the most talented "talker" of all parrots. Only the Greater Hill Mynah (a non-parrot) is superior in its ability to mimic the human voice and other sounds so accurately.

The Grey is much more a one person parrot than most others, and may take a dislike to a given sex. They are far less outgoing than the Amazons in their willingness to "perform" when strangers are present. They are less trustworthy of strangers, and if not tame will literally growl at you when approached. For some people these characteristics make them undesirable, to others it is the very essence of what a Grey is all about. A good Grey can be an amazing bird, which is why they are held in such high esteem. Their life span can exceed 60 years.

SENEGAL PARROT—*POICEPHALUS SENEGALUS* 23CM (9IN)

This small parrot will cost less than half the price of the Grey. It is one of nine species in the genus that are indigenous to Africa, and it has been a popular pet for a few centuries. It has rather dull head colors, being a gray with a black beak, but it has bright orange-yellow on its chest, and a light green neck and upper chest. It may learn to speak a few words, and if acquired as a youngster makes a delightful pet. Being small, it is not too noisy, nor destructive. If it has a drawback it's that its orange eye against the dark plumage gives it a somewhat sinister look that might intimidate some people, the more so because, like others in the genus, it has quite a large beak.

The small Senegal parrot has a very sinister look about it, however, it proves to be a very sweet and loving bird.

ASIATIC PARAKEETS—GENUS *PSITTACULA* 33-50CM (13-20IN)

The parrots of this genus are often known as the ring-necked parakeets for the ring of color that either encircles their head, or for their obvious half circle mustache of black. They are generally regarded as being more suited to the aviary than as a caged pet. When acquired as youngsters they do make delightful pets but require a large cage to accommodate their long tail feathers.

Although the basic color is a medium to light green, they all have other colors in their plumage. Those, such as the Plum-headed, *P. cyanocephala*, are quite exquisitely colored, and all have

The Bourke's Parakeet is one of the more popular Australian parakeets found on the market. They display lovely pink and blue coloring especially visible in flight.

when in numbers, but less so than the conures.

AUSTRALIAN PARAKEETS

As a group, the Australian parakeets have to be the world's most colorful and, in many ways, desirable parrots for the aviarist. As a general rule, they do not make good cage pets when compared to many other species you could purchase for the same or less money. Prices range from modest to extremely expensive, but even in the lower priced species you get a lot of bird for your money, and there are many mutational colors. They are less destructive to their aviaries than are most other parrots and longtailed parakeets, and are

The Turquoisine Parakeet is not as common as some of the other Australian parakeets. Its iridescent blue and green colors cannot be matched by other species.

smooth immaculate plumage when in good feather. Some have large red or black beaks, and others have moderate to small beaks. The Alexandrine, *P. eupatria*, one of the larger species, makes an extremely nice pet being more "parrot-like" than many longtailed parakeets.

The Indian ringneck, *P. krameri*, though rather plainly colored, has been a popular cage and aviary bird for many years. This has been helped by its modest price. However, in its numerous mutational forms it can be a breathtakingly stunning bird—as are other ringnecks in which mutations, such as blue, lutino, and albino are seen. The ringnecks are definitely recommended to the aviculturist who wants to specialize in color forms. They can be noisy quieter, some having pleasant call notes.

Long recognized and appreciated for their beauty in Britain and mainland Europe where they are extensively bred, they have steadily gained devotees in the USA. They can only become more and more popular as they are seen by more people.

Among the less costly species you should check out are those of the genus *Neophema*. This genus includes the beautifully colored Splendid Grass Parakeet, *N. splendida*, the ever popular Bourke's, *N. bourkii*, the charming Turquoisine, *N. pulchella*, and the Elegant, *N. elegans*. Each is

The Moustache Parakeet is a ground feeder that will do well in an outdoor aviary. Be sure to provide a heat source for these beautiful parrots if they are to be housed outdoors during the colder climates.

There are many mutational varieties of the Ring-necked parakeet. This is a lutino, however, blues and albinos are also available.

sexually dimorphic, and in size they are all under 24cm (9.5in). They are close relatives of the budgerigar.

They represent an excellent investment for any breeder, and all are very well established in captivity (in which all will have been bred, unless you are living in Australia). You may have to seek these out from a breeder because they are not a species seen too often in pet shops.

If you like really vivid colors, then the larger Eastern or Red Rosella, *Platycerus eximus*, is the bird for you. With its red head, white throat, yellow lower chest, and yellow and black wings over a green tail, they just don't come any better! For good measure the wing edges are blue. It is larger than the grass parakeets at 31cm (12in), and is by far the most freely available of the numerous and stunningly beautiful broadtails of the Australian continent.

SOUTH AMERICAN CONURES

The many conures (parakeets) of South America have been to American parrot enthusiasts what the Australian and Asiatic species have been to the British and other Europeans. More outgoing in their character, many make very desirable pets. A few are extremely

The Jendaya Conure makes a nice pet for someone that can withstand a bit of noise. These birds are not known for their ability to talk, however, they prove to be very friendly and outgoing.

colorful and majestic to behold. If the conures have a drawback it's that they can be rather raucous, their screeching being heard quite some distance away. This makes them rather less suitable as aviary birds in populated communities, added to which they are much more destructive to woodwork than their Australian counterparts.

Most are kept as pets, and the more readily available species will cost you about half the price, or less, of an Amazon parrot or African Grey. In looks, some are rather like dwarf macaws, but lack the large bare facial area of these other South American psittacines.

With its golden yellow head and body plumage, contrasting with green wings and black beak, the Jendaya Conure, *Aratinga jandaya*, is one of a trio of very impressive conures. The related subspecies, the Sun Conure, *A. solstitialis*, has more yellow in its plumage, but will cost you more money, as will the larger Queen of Bavaria's Conure, *Aratinga guarouba*, which is a true avian gem. Compared to these vivid parrots most other conures are plain by comparison, but make no less pets, and will be less expensive. The little Petz's Conure (with a horn colored beak), *A. canicularis*, and the rather similar looking Golden-crowned Conure (with black beak), *A. aurea*, are only about 24cm (9.5in) tall so are more easily catered for than the large neotropical parakeets.

Much larger at 31cm (12in), the Nanday Conure has been a favorite parrot for many years. The head and beak are black, the rest of the plumage green, except for some blue on the chest, and red thighs. It is a ready breeder in pairs, or on a colony system, but very noisy. However, hand reared chicks are far quieter and truly delightful companions to own. If you decide to obtain any of this group of birds as a pet, make every effort to purchase either a hand-reared baby, or one straight from the nest.

MACAWS 31–100CM (12-34IN)

These giants of the parrot world are truly impressive. Colorful, highly intelligent, confiding, and always imposing, they are nonetheless suited to very few households or aviaries. Their beaks are enormous and capable of tremendous destruction. Their voices can be ear shattering, especially in the confines of a house room, while their accommodation will be highly expensive. A bite from most parrots can be very painful—one from these birds would be very serious.

These remarks apply to the larger macaw species, such as the Scarlet, the Blue and Yellow, and the Military macaws, it is not always appreciated that there are some much smaller species that can be purchased. Cassin's or Yellow Collared, *Ara auricollis*, is one example. It is a mere 38cm

Many different conure species exist and they range from dull and drab coloration to most vivid. Conures require housing that is slightly larger than that for a cockatiel, however, this must be much stronger to withstand their beak strength.

(16in), but every inch as much a macaw as its larger cousins. A reliable breeding bird, this is an attractive green parrot with a black forehead and beak contrasting against the white bare skin around the eyes.

The Severe, Hahn's, and Noble macaws are other available species that can be recommended, and which are no more costly than the more desirable Amazons. At only 31cm (12in) the last two species named are the smallest of this famous group of parrots.

AMAZON PARROTS—GENUS *AMAZONA* 25-35CM(10-14IN)

For many parrot enthusiasts, an Amazon parrot is the one they aspire to own. Extroverted, talented talkers, amusing, and very companionable, these basically green, short tailed birds are perhaps the epitome of what the pet parrot is all about. Today, many are bred in aviaries and birdrooms, so there is not a problem in obtaining hand fed babies—and these are the ones you should obtain.

Of course, these desirable birds are quite expensive. You will get little change from $1,000 for the more sought after species. But, with a lifespan comparable to your own, this is really not so much for what you are getting. A word of caution: these birds, especially when they are very tame, can at times become very aggressive, not hesitating to bite. This is especially so with males in breeding condition. Like the African Grey, they can also be rather selective in whom they will take a liking to, usually preferring one sex over the other. Their high intelligence means they do get belligerent when they cannot get their own way. They need firm, but gentle and loving owners who will not become intimidated by their bossy antics! There are 27 species, but many of these are rarely seen. Among the more popular is the perennial favorite the Blue-fronted, *A. aestiva*, and the rather similar Orange-winged, *A. amazonica*.

The species *A. ochrocephala*, includes a number of subspecies that are sold under a variety of names, such as Mexican Yellow-head, Double Yellow-head, Panama, Marajo, Magna, and Yellow-naped. The common feature is the yellow on the head, which is variable in its extent.

COCKATOOS—GENUS *CACATUA* 31-50CM (12-20IN)

Instantly recognizable with their plume-like crests and, in most species, white plumage, the cockatoos have deservingly gained a reputation for being among the most intelligent and confiding of parrots. Very long-lived, they are the most expensive of the parrots from which you are likely to choose. However, as with the macaws, you are advised to admire rather than buy one.

These birds are extremely demanding on their owners. If you cannot devote a great deal of time to them you will quickly be aware of the error in acquiring one, as very many owners soon do. They will start to pluck their feathers, chew on your furniture, and screech at the top of their voices whenever you are not around. Cages and aviaries suited to these birds will be very costly, but it is the time that they need devoted to them that is the main reason why they prove unsuitable to many owners.

If you feel you have the time and the money to obtain a cockatoo you should commence with one of the smaller species, such as the Lesser Sulphur-crested, *C. sulphurea*. It is imperative that, as with all medium to large parrots, it is given as much time out of its cage as possible. It will otherwise quickly become a dejected and very unhappy bird. Do remember that all parrots are highly sociable avians that will be negatively effected if they are denied the company of their own kind, or a suitable substitute—you and your family.

The birds discussed in this chapter are but a sampling of various species and groups that are readily available. Before purchasing any which appeal, you are strongly advised to purchase a book devoted to the species, or the group it is in. This will give you the extra information you should have before obtaining the parrot. Such a book is available from a very extensive listing published by T.F.H. Publications Inc.